HONG KONG

A MOMENT IN TIME

HONG

A MOMENT IN TIME

KONG

To John and Rhona,

PRODUCED BY
Tim Nutt & Chris Bale

Chris Bale.

THE CHINESE UNIVERSITY PRESS

Hong Kong
June 1997

ISBN: 962-201-772-X

THE CHINESE UNIVERSITY PRESS
The Chinese University of Hong Kong,
Sha Tin, N.T., Hong Kong.
Fax: (852) 2603 6692
      (852) 2603 7355
E-mail: cup@cuhk.edu.hk
Web-site: http://www.cuhk.edu.hk/cupress/w1.htm
Printed in Hong Kong

Photography:
Tim Nutt, John Lambon, Ian Stevens

Text:
Chris Bale

Original art work:
Fang Zhaoling, Chung Wah Nan, John Au

Calligraphy and verse for each theme:
Chung Wah Nan

Design:
Tim Nutt, The Chinese University Press

Promotion:
Valeria Nutt, The Chinese University Press

Production:
The Chinese University Press

Contents

Theme One

- **HARBOUR**
- **JUNKS**
- **FESTIVALS**

Interview:
Fang Zhaoling

Theme Two

- **CONTRASTS**
- **MARKETS**
- **STREET SCENES**

Interview:
Doris Lau

Theme Three

- **BUILDINGS**
- **HOUSING**
- **PAVILION**

Interview:
Chung Wah Nan

Theme Four

- **TRANSPORT**
- **DEVELOPMENT**
- **N.T. VILLAGES**

Interview:
Sir David Akers-Jones

Theme Five

- **IMAGES**
- **SPORTS**
- **ACTION**

Interview:
Jackie Chan

Introduction

Tim Nutt
Chris Bale

 You'd better explain yourself, Tim, tell people how this all started.

 Well, I was walking in the hills one Sunday afternoon last summer and suddenly thought to myself that I must do something to mark 1997. I mean, I've lived here for twenty years and for most of that time Hong Kong has been obsessed with 1997. It's such a fascinating moment in history, so very focused.

 But there are plenty of books about 1997. We didn't need another one from you.

 No, I realised that nobody would want to read the thoughts of Chairman Nutt. But then I thought that if I asked hundreds of friends for their thoughts, we'd have a book that really would be unique, showing how Hong Kong people see their city, reflecting their feelings and memories. So I sent out hundreds of questionnaires—and, in a moment of weakness, solicited your help to write a few words.

 I can't believe you know so many people from so many different backgrounds. Some were born and bred here, some came to work, some simply visited, some have now moved away, but they all contributed.

 And every photo in the book has been inspired by one of their comments.

The trouble is there were so many images and ideas that it's been impossible to represent all of them. It's like the problem you faced in deciding who to interview.

 Choosing ten people from a city of six million isn't easy, so I decided to talk only to people we knew, people whose own stories also say something about the story of Hong Kong.

Christine Fang was talking about being a community worker in Kowloon, and she said to me: "Each night you go out and you look up at these public housing blocks, and they are full of so many lights—and each light is a story." That's how I see the book—each picture, each interview, each quotation tells a story.

 It's been a great experience because people have been so eager to help. Many of them have taken time to think about Hong Kong, and we've included some of their answers as quotations. My old friend John Lambon contributed a lot of stunning photographs, and the team at Chinese University Press took care of design and production with their usual skill and enthusiasm.

 Typical of you to forget your wife. We'd never have done this without Valeria's patience and support.

 Typical of you to humiliate me in print. But the hardest thing about this

book has been trying to present so many ideas in a roughly logical way. It's not a book you can present in chapters, but we have grouped photographs together around various themes. With each of the people interviewed, we have tried to show a mosaic of images which are relevant to that particular person. I hope the result is a book which people can open at any page and have fun with.

 Why did you want to include children's paintings?

 Because children see things so clearly and their use of colour is so bold. They add an extra dimension to the book. When you consider that these children are all either physically or mentally handicapped, I think their talents are remarkable.

 You know, reading the answers to your questionnaire, what really struck me was how much people love Hong Kong. When you and I first came here twenty years ago, this place was

either a bolt hole from China or a stepping stone to somewhere else, but that has changed. Chinese friends are now proud to call themselves Hongkongers and expatriate friends feel privileged to live here. Of course, we all moan about this or that, but not a single person was negative about Hong Kong. Not one.

 Which is really where I started from—wanting to celebrate this marvellous city and to

mark a momentous time in its history. The book is not involved with the politics of 1997 and we're not implying that 1997 marks the end of anything or the start of anything.

 Simply that it is a moment in time.

 Trust you to want the last word.

山河 見今章情

Evoking rivers and mountains to express feelings.

"A deep green forest of pyramidal peaks, with stark high-rise factories and apartment buildings rising like columns of white crystal at their base."

"An elegant British tea party watching a Chinese festival."

"My first impression? As we sailed through Lai Yue Mun, the incredible vista at dawn, as the most beautiful harbour in the world opened up before us."

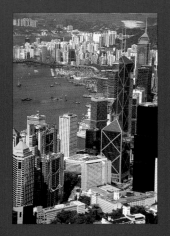

"The night view of Hong Kong Island—
a mountain of sparkling jewels."

"A splendid and beautiful place, with its
winding roads and soaring buildings."

"First impressions? Four-storeyed buildings along the harbour—pirates in the Pearl Estuary."

3

Fang Zhaoling
方 召 麐

On the first day of 1997, Fang Zhaoling completed two paintings and six pieces of calligraphy. At eighty-three, Hong Kong's most celebrated artist is at the height of her powers.

Her Southern Mountain Studio, above Deepwater Bay, is also her home. The dining table is covered with inks, brushes and seals, paintings are laid out to dry on the living room floor and even her bedroom is cluttered with scrolls.

"Whenever it is possible," she says, "I must hold a brush. As Rousseau said, life is creation."

Mrs Fang has lived boldly. She was widowed at an early age and left with eight young children, but nothing could deflect her from a passion for painting. She spent fifteen years learning to paint flowers and birds in the classical Chinese style, but then discovered the

European masters— Chagall, Matisse and Picasso. She has absorbed many influences but surrendered to none.

"I decided that I have to walk my own way," she says firmly.

She has travelled the world, living in many places and visiting many more, but now in Hong Kong she feels that she has come home. Over the past couple of years she has produced many paintings on the theme of Peaceful Transition, reflecting her supreme confidence in Hong Kong's future.

"Everybody worries about Hong Kong's future, but I don't. Tomorrow will be better."

A number of her recent paintings bear the characters 艱苦創造

(hardship leads to creation)—a reflection not only of Hong Kong's development but of her own struggles. For there were times when, as an

unknown artist in England, she would happily sell a painting for a few pounds because she needed to buy food. Visitors to her studio home would find discarded works torn up and hung in the bathroom as toilet paper.

Today, her paintings fetch US$40,000 and more. There is to be a permanent display of Fang Zhaoling masterpieces at the University of Hong Kong and she has plenty of unseen works rolled up at home. Her needs are modest and she need never paint another stroke.

Yet every morning she is seated at her table by seven-o-clock. She picks up a newly bought brush and turns its thick bristles in the black ink. The paper is stretched in front of her and she pauses for a moment, visualising the characters, deciding the scale. Then she plunges into her work, moving the brush swiftly and strongly, her hand perfectly steady. A piece of calligraphy may take only a few minutes to complete but it is executed with vigour and purpose.

"Even when you reach old age," she says, "you are still young. Tomorrow you can climb another summit."

香港的明天更
加繁榮穩定更為
幸福更加努力建設 丁丑

平穩過渡
一九九六年方召麐

Hong Kong will be more prosperous and more stable.
The people will be happier and will put more effort on
building a better tomorrow.

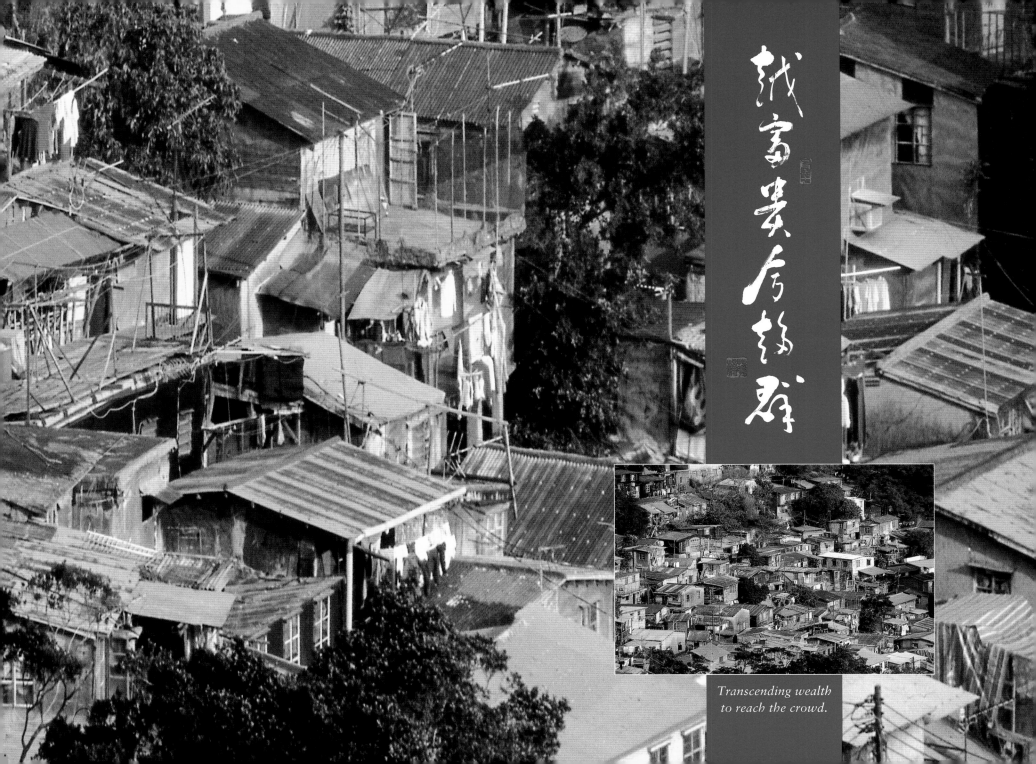

越富貴存勁群

*Transcending wealth
to reach the crowd.*

"Energy will keep Hong Kong moving into whatever future lies ahead."

"Culturally divided but materialistically united."

"Everything is polarised by the intensity of life. Extremes of peace and chaos, wealth and poverty, density and open space exist within a few miles of each other."

"Every street holds a secret."

"Contrasts at every turn—rich and poor, dark and light, noise and peace, high and low, confined and spacious, fast and slow."

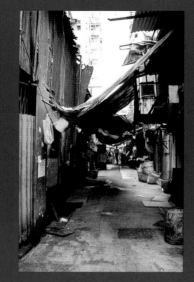

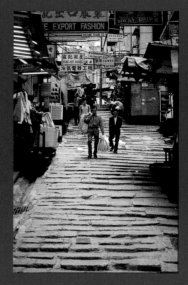

Doris Lau
劉　群　章

235 Shanghai Street, Yau Ma Tei was demolished years ago. The site is now a children's playground. Nobody remembers the dingy old three-storeyed tenement building which used to stand there — nobody, that is, except Doris Lau, who spent the first fifteen years of her life there. She cannot forget.

The top floor flat of number 235 was divided into three cubicles. The ones at the back and the front of the building had more light, but the Lau family had the one in the middle because it was cheaper. Nine people — father, mother, grandmother and six children — lived in a single room of less than one hundred square feet.

Three families shared a small kitchen. Twenty-four people took turns to bath in the kitchen. The toilet was also in the kitchen and a night soil woman called each night to empty the bucket.

"We cooked with wood and my job was to cut the wood into small pieces and stack them neatly under the bed — well, under one side of the bed because I had to sleep under there as well.

"My mother would rather go hungry than borrow money but when we didn't have any money she would borrow rice from the neighbours. She would add a bit of salt and a bit of oil and that would be a meal."

"We never had new clothes at New Year. I had a primary school teacher, Miss Ma, who used to give me all her old shoes and clothes. And yet until I went to secondary school I never felt that I was ill provided for. I never had a toy in my life, but I was quite happy playing in the streets. Now my daughter is at university and she has a bedroom full of stuffed toys. I just can't relate to that. What does she need them for?

"People were much nicer then. They reacted to one another in a more direct and simple way. When I was doing my secondary school entrance exam, the son of a widow in one of the other cubicles helped me with my English. His English actually wasn't very good but he worked for a tailor in Tsim Sha Tsui and so he had to deal with tourists. He helped me a lot but we never paid him any money — not even a free meal or a small present. Can you imagine that happening today?"

The little girl from Shanghai Street excelled in her secondary school entrance exam and arrived at St Paul's Secondary School, among girls who came from much wealthier homes and who spoke much better English.

"On the first day at St Paul's I couldn't even get the timetable down because I didn't know what the teacher was talking about. We had to go up to the teacher and tell her our English name, but my name was Lau Kwan Cheung. I remember thinking: 'Quick, quick, quick, think of an English name,' and the only one I knew was Doris Day because my father loved Doris Day. So I became Doris."

She soon realised that her family was poor.

"I remember I was using cheap Chung Hwa pencils, the red ones, made in China, but the other kids were using a brand called Venus, which were orange. Of course, I felt the difference."

Today, the little girl who was embarrassed by the colour of her pencils has become a sophisticated and successful public relations executive. She dresses in chic outfits, flies business class, cooks French cuisine and has a passion for fine wines. She speaks four languages, is married to an Englishman and crosses cultures with accomplished ease. She is the epitome of the modern international career woman.

And yet ...

"When I'm out of Hong Kong, what I really miss is the food. Not smart restaurants but *da bin lo* (hot pot) and *dai pai dong* (street kitchens). I love Hong Kong's wet markets."

And when life is particularly hard, she goes where her grandma used to go—to Wong Tai Sin temple.

"When grandma had a stroke a few years ago I went to see Wong Tai Sin and told him that if he made sure my grandma was okay I would go back and give him a roast pig—which I did."

Although she has lived in Paris, Taipei and Singapore and has an apartment in London, she still yearns for Hong Kong.

"Obviously, because it's my home and I have so much emotional past here, but also because this is a place like no other, the only place on this planet that seems to be constantly pushing itself forward, driving itself on."

That description applies also to her. Like many Hong Kong people of her generation, Doris Lau has got to where she is today by struggling, driving other people hard and herself even harder. She has a consuming need to prove herself to herself.

"I know it sounds stoical, but if you ask me whether I would rather be born into poverty or be born rich, I would choose the same again. I have no regrets. If I go to Yau Ma Tei now and walk down Shanghai Street, of course it's changed—but I still remember and I still have this swelling in my heart."

Dreaming of ancient wood for beams and columns.

"A seething city, reinventing and reproducing itself as though there may be no tomorrow."

"Hong Kong is a privilege of the twentieth century."

"The relative peace of Sai Kung provides a much needed contrast to a busy working day in the city."

"Concrete forest."

"Hong Kong changes too quickly."

"A dynamic place, where projects and dreams are realised and where making money isn't a sin."

"Hong Kong gets the buildings it deserves."

28

Chung Wah Nan
鍾 華 楠

Hong Kong delights builders but disappoints architects. There are plenty of buildings to design, of course, but developers are interested in money, not style.

"We lack patrons," says Chung Wah Nan, doyen of local architects. "There is nobody who wants a piece of architecture. If they do, it's their interpretation of architecture, which is completely not in touch with this time and this culture. It's just their fancy, a childish dream or something they have seen abroad."

After working here for more than thirty years, he concludes: "Maybe out of every ten buildings that can satisfy my clients, I have one that can satisfy me in my own mind."

Chung Wah Nan is a small man who is larger than life. A human firework. He sits behind his enormous desk, wearing a bright red sweater, wisps of pipe smoke wafting around his head. His eyes are bright, he speaks quickly and often explodes with laughter. He does not seem like a man who is disappointed nine times out of ten.

"Hong Kong architects are excellent at dealing with 1,001 regulations, maximising the development potential of a site and still coming up with good buildings," he says. "They are good buildings—but they are not regional buildings."

There's the rub. Mr Chung's great passion is for Hong Kong and China to develop their own architectural styles, using the best technology and latest materials to express classical Chinese concepts in a modern way.

"The great composers like Brahms, Bartok, Janacek were all familiar with their native music and they interpreted it in a way that appealed to people everywhere. China lacks that step. It's either Western or Chinese. Very little energy has been spent on making Chinese culture international. The only one who has been able to do it is the chef—he alone can interpret Chinese food to international tastes."

The man who designed Hong Kong landmarks such as the City University, the old Peak Tower and Tregunter chooses as his most satisfying project a set of pavilions in public parks in Wanchai and north Kowloon, which were inspired by the ancient Chinese nine-square planning grid.

"They are really worthless to others, but to me they are buildings that represent a philosophy. You play in a pavilion as a child, you experience your first love there, you say goodbye there. They are totally

without function—when the typhoon blows they don't even keep the rain out—but in terms of philosophy, in terms of simplicity of structure, they have everything.

"If you ask me what are the representative buildings of Hong Kong, it's not the buildings along the Central waterfront—if you took out the old Supreme Court building you could be anywhere. No, it's our

public housing estates. Those I like and I think we've done a really good job on them."

Apart from designing buildings himself, Mr Chung is a renowned writer on architecture and an enthusiastic calligrapher, although he is quick to play down his accomplishments.

"If you can't design, you write, and if you can't paint, you do calligraphy," he says, bursting into laughter again.

"Architecture is a disciplined profession.

You can let your imagination run wild, but a building has to stand up. It has to be ventilated. It has to be used. People have to live in it or make profit out of it. Architecture is a way of life.

"Calligraphy is a way of expression. It's how, after some wine, I can express myself. That's why I am very fond of the grass style of calligraphy. Some strokes can be long, some can be short. In architecture, you serve a lot of people but in calligraphy you serve yourself."

In his thinking on both architecture and calligraphy, Chung Wah Nan draws his inspiration from ancient Chinese culture—even if his clients are more concerned with twentieth century economics.

山高水長源無盡
柳綠桃紅又一春

Long waterfalls from high mountains flow from inexhaustible sources.
Young green willow leaves and pink peach blossoms announce yet another spring.

去了好枝红也老原去山是几

東風來了輕鬆

*The east wind blows
and brings a sense
of ease.*

"The focus is always straight ahead, living for tomorrow which everyone believes, or wants to believe, will be better than today—more rice in your bowl, more money under the mattress, more flats, more sons, more grandsons."

36

"Hong Kong is home — and has been since the moment I arrived."

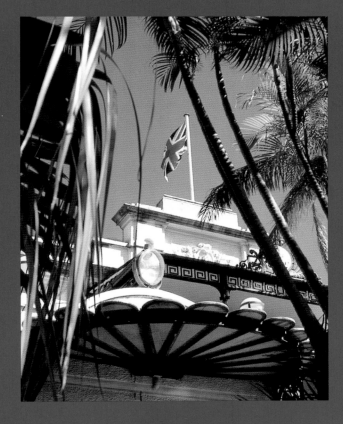

"Flying in so close that you can not only see families eating but see what they are eating."

"Packed in on a bus to Pak Tin!"

"Taxis are only abundant when you don't want one."

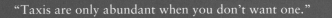

Sir David Akers-Jones
鍾 逸 傑 爵 士

Sir David Akers-Jones spent his working life building the future of Hong Kong.

Although he rose to become Chief Secretary and Acting Governor, he is chiefly identified with the development of the New Territories, a scheme that fundamentally changed the physical appearance and social fabric of Hong Kong. Vegetable fields and pig farms were cleared to make way for seven new towns which are now home to hundreds and thousands of people. The scale of Hong Kong was changed forever.

"Hong Kong today is in total contrast to the place I came to in 1957," he reflects. "There has been a progression year by year. You can mark it off like the rings on an oak tree.

"Back in those days there was a great divide between Hong Kong Island and Kowloon. It wasn't just the difficulty of moving from one side of the harbour to the other. It was the attitude of people on Hong Kong Island towards Kowloon. It wasn't until 1966 that the first solicitor went to work in Kowloon—and he was regarded as a very strange fellow. There were people in the government, quite senior officials, who had never been to places like Cheung Chau."

As a district officer, the young Akers-Jones

ventured further afield. In his first year he walked to every village on the outlying islands.

"The nice thing at that time was that we were dealing with village people whose daily lives were centred around the village. The work involved the passing of the seasons— the planting of vegetables, the planting of rice."

No longer.

"The quality of Hong Kong people has changed—not necessarily for better or for worse, but it has changed. I think urban people are now much more aware of, and much more influenced by, the West. Everyone in Hong Kong now travels. Your taxi driver takes his holiday in foreign countries.

"The closeness of the community, when everyone knew everyone, the familiarity of family and friends and neighbours—that has been lost. Sometimes in high-rise buildings people do not even know who lives next door to them.

"But we must value what we have gained. For instance, we have gained a much more sophisticated cultural life. I remember when the cultural life of Hong Kong was confined to an annual performance of Gilbert and Sullivan in Lugard Hall and an occa-

sional concert by a scratch orchestra conducted by Solly Bard.

"Hong Kong has developed two faces—one is capitalist and one is socialist. The capitalist half pays for the socialist half. By 'socialist' I mean practically free primary and secondary education, heavily subsi-

dised tertiary education, practically free medical services and heavily subsidised public housing."

But progress has not always been smooth and well planned.

"We have had to move so fast in terms of economic development that we have not had time to reflect sufficiently on, and to preserve, what is good in the present. For instance, we were completely overwhelmed by the revolution

in shipping. We were used to ships mooring in the harbour and at the godowns along the Kowloon Peninsula, but suddenly we had to handle enormous container ships. The only place to put the port was in Kwai Chung but Kwai Chung had no land. The wharves were built on a fringe of reclamation but all the empty boxes spilled out into the New Territories.

"So gradually the whole of the New Territories was changed from being

smiling paddy fields to being the detritus of the towns. I've got a painting upstairs which I did in 1968 of the Sek Kong valley, and the valley floor is yellow. Look at it now!"

Yet despite his regrets about the loss of some spectacularly beautiful countryside, Sir David does not doubt that Hong Kong's frenetic development has been for the better and that this remains the best place to live. Unlike most colonial officials, he did not retire to grow roses in Sussex but stayed on, tending his precious orchids at Tsing Lung Tau.

"I think it is the roundness of the Hong Kong experience," he explains. "You can really live a full life here in every sense. You can take a superficial interest in Chinese culture, enjoy Chinese food and the comforts of living in Hong Kong, or you can make China and the Chinese a lifetime's study."

His own lifetime's study has led him to one conclusion about the people of Hong Kong, one which holds true despite all the changes of the past forty years.

"The Chinese are not alone in this, but they do cherish their 'Chineseness'. They have a tremendous regard for their own ways of doing things and a conviction about their ability to overcome any challenge — business, health, education, anything. They are Chinese of the essence."

勤骨勞今榮記

Working to the bone in order to be successful.

"A unique, multi-national pin prick on the map which gives everybody a chance at life."

"One can achieve more at work and socially in one day here than most people achieve in a week elsewhere."

48

"Making money—and having a good time doing it!"

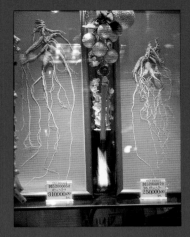

"A crisp $500 note."

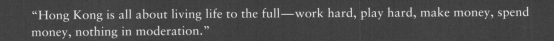

"Hong Kong is all about living life to the full—work hard, play hard, make money, spend money, nothing in moderation."

49

Jackie Chan
成 龍

There is one Hong Kong person whose name and face are known all over the world—Jackie Chan.

Yet ironically Hong Kong's most famous son shoots all his movies overseas and earns most of his money from overseas screenings. Hong Kong is home but it's no longer big enough.

"Hong Kong is so small. Development so quick. The roads are tiny, even the rivers are getting smaller. There's no place to let me do a lot of fighting scenes, chasing scenes, explosions. Even you do them it's illegal. If you tell the police, they say No."

Does he miss Hong Kong when he's filming overseas?

"Very much. I call Hong Kong every day and I get a fax from Hong Kong every day with all the news headlines—that's very important. I miss atmosphere, food, friends.

"Hong Kong is the most exciting place. In the States, if you want to have three meetings you need a week. In Hong Kong, we have ten meetings in a day. You can have dinner early in the morning or in the middle of the night— we're twenty-four hours. Shopping is very cheap. It's just a very exciting place—and very pretty at night.

"I was born here. Not just my house is my home, the whole of Hong Kong is my home. Even the policeman says: Hey, *dai gor* (big brother). Everybody treats me like a friend."

Jackie has won friends from Mongkok to Morocco, from Madras to Miami.

"Right now, the most important market is the States. Then Germany, then Japan. In Asia, it's Korea, Taiwan and then Hong Kong. Hong Kong market is actually very small."

His films are ideal for a diverse international audience, relying not on story or dialogue but on action. Body language says it all, whether it's a comic expression or one of his incredible stunts.

"They don't have to hear Jackie Chan talk, they just have to see Jackie Chan move."

The superstar's schedule is ridiculous.

"Every night I have to check with my manager what will happen tomorrow. He tells me: 'OK, you have to get up at six thirty. Dress up because you've got a photo shoot. Then you'll have two hours in the gym, then six interviews.' He's got my programme for the whole month in a computer. Sometimes he says: 'See you at the airport tomorrow morning at nine.' When I get there I say: 'OK, where are we going?' Yeah, you're right, I'm

not in control. Except on the film—then I am in control."

He is quick to acknowledge that fame has brought him great wealth.

"We're living the rich life. Cold—turn on the heater. Hot—turn on the aircon. I want to go to Taiwan but it's not good timing— there's a private jet coming. They give me a sandwich.

I think: 'I'm just eating a sandwich.' But the sandwich came from The Peninsula!"

It was not always so.

"When I was young I was helped by the American Red Cross. They gave me clothes. One day I said to the Father: 'Thank you.' He said: 'Don't thank me. One day you will have the strength, you will help somebody.' That's why I started the Jackie Chan Charitable Foundation.

"I like money, everyone likes money, but I don't want to get more, more, more. Like Li Ka Shing— too much money! Keep so much money is useless. I want to keep earning and keep spending. I hope when I die I will owe the bank a billion, billion dollars!"

Jackie has paid a price for stardom but harbours no regrets.

"I lost my family, my own private life. A lot of things I like I can't do. I want to be a racing driver. Cannot. Nobody lets me go to disco or karaoke, not even my own Planet Hollywood. Last year I only spent fifteen days with my family. My parents are in Australia and I want to be with them—not for one day, at least one week. But cannot.

"But my family understand that I can do many great things. I can visit an old people's home for a hundred old men. I can visit a thousand children in hospital. I can do entertainment for a billion people."

身心俱疲，為家計。

Exhausting body and mind for the family's well-being.

"There will always be a place in my heart for the Chinese people of Hong Kong."

"Very old ladies unhurriedly carefully choosing fruit."

"Striving to improve within a family unit, so that the younger generation can have better opportunities."

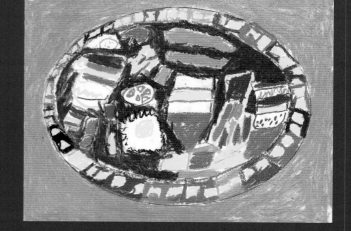

"The wok is a remarkably well designed cooking utensil."

"The safest place in the world to work, to live and to enjoy life."

"Fish beyond all imagining."

"Smartness of school children in their uniforms."

Going out in a junk and eating at the pigeon restaurant on amma. My guest said it was the happiest day of her life."

Leung Kwok Lin Choi

梁 郭 蓮 彩

"Hong Kong."

Kwok Lin Choi had heard the name but it meant little to her. In a small town in southern China, she rose every morning at four-o-clock and climbed the hillside to gather firewood for the stove. She watched her mother work long, backbreaking hours as a coolie, trying to earn enough money to feed three children. Life was a raw struggle for survival.

Her father was working overseas, ostensibly earning money for the family but actually spending most of it on drink and opium for himself. It was her mother, a tiny woman of enormous resilience and strength, who kept the family together.

"She was the best mother in the world. We were so poor but she kept us alive."

At the age of twenty-two Miss Kwok became Mrs Leung, and in 1964 the family moved to Hong Kong with three small children, to live in a stone hut in Hoi Pa, Tsuen Wan. The hut measured 100 square feet and had no light, no electricity, no toilet, no water, no kitchen. The rent was $40 per month. Her husband earned about $5 a day as a carpenter but they spent $3 to $4 a day on food.

"The main problem was poverty. We had no money and every day I was just thinking about how to get food."

Did the children ever go to bed hungry?

"No. We always managed to eat something, but sometimes it was only plain congee."

Did she ever regret leaving China?

"No. Never. Life there was even harder. In Hong Kong, you always have a chance."

She pauses, silently reviewing her life. Then she sighs and adds, "Looking backwards, the strongest image is of those hard times in China. The best thing that ever happened to me was leaving China and coming to Hong Kong."

Two more children were born and after a few years the family moved into a new public housing estate at Shek Yam, Kwai Chung.

"That day," she remembers, "was like winning the Mark Six."

Mr Leung earned the family income while Mrs Leung stayed at home to look after the children. Everything was done for the sake of the children.

"I remember one day we all went to a restaurant. We ordered five dishes

and the children ate all of them. We had no chance to eat anything and the waiter asked us why not. I said, 'Well, it's quite common that all the food goes to the children.'"

Did she have any dreams for herself?

"I never thought about spending money on myself. I was always worried about getting enough money for the children. All my dreams were children, children and children."

Gradually, the dreams began to come true. To his

parents' immense pride, second son graduated from the Chinese University and became a doctor. Second daughter graduated from the University of Hong Kong. First son married and first grandson was born.

So today, at sixty-three, Leung Kwok Lin Choi is a contented woman. The years of struggle have brought their reward. She smiles and says that Hong Kong, where all these

dreams came true, is the best place in the world.

What in particular does she like about it?

" *Yan ching mei* (the warmth of human relationships). My neighbours are very helpful," she says. "And the food. Buying food is very convenient."

All five children have married and are doing well. Four of them have bought their own apartments. There are nine grandchildren, ranging from twelve years to twelve days old, and Mrs Leung says her role now is to be "on standby", ready to go to whichever child or grandchild needs her. She enjoys shuttling between the five young families and her only wish is for her grandchildren to "grow up healthy and go in the right way."

She smiles again and says, "Really, I have no more worries." But then she remembers there is one. Her mother, living with her in Kwai Chung, is eighty-eight and in failing health. Now Mrs Leung must care for the woman who, half a century ago in China, struggled so hard to care for her. She is repaying a debt of love and respect to the woman who first showed her what it means to be a mother.

方寸守今達法

"Textures? The calloused rub of work-worn hands and the cool smoothness of well-worn jade."

"Bargaining — and once the deal is struck, excellent execution."

"Unique image? A gold toothed 'coolie' shuffling along the street while talking into a mobile."

"Negotiations in freezing air conditioned shops call for frequent rushes outside to warm up."

"Busy working, busy socialising, busy doing nothing."

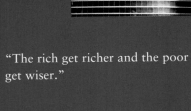

"The rich get richer and the poor get wiser."

"A place where the past is pushed into the future and the future is pushed into the past."

"Favourite Hong Kong places? My office, my bath tub, my bed."

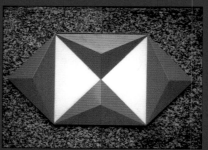

John Au

區　賢　浩

John Au must have been about fifteen at the time. His father, who ran a family printing business, called him in and asked him straight: "What are you going to do when you leave school?" The boy had no idea, so his father made a suggestion: "Think about going to America to study graphic design."

The chairman of the Hong Kong Designers Association smiles at the memory.

"I don't know what he saw in me," he says. "I certainly didn't see it in myself, but I felt tremendously energised by his suggestion."

 John duly graduated from the California Institute of Arts, worked for design studios in New York and grew up. Then, after six years away, he came home and worked for top designer Henry Steiner. Three years later,

in a corner of his father's factory, he opened John Au Design Associates.

So what is the John Au style? East Meets West?

"I am the kind of designer who tries to solve the problem with the right solution. I am not a stylist. I am not trying to make a big statement that every bit of my work must show East meeting West. I see

myself as a doctor. I don't just have one pill called 'East Meets West' and, whatever is wrong with the patient, I give him the same pill. If one client needs a plain paper cover, that's fine, that's what I give him."

He has not returned to New York in sixteen years and relishes the fact that he is now designing for his own community.

"A few years ago I did The Community Chest's annual report and that was a very nice thing to do, very meaningful. I grew up with The Community Chest, it's like a part of me, and now I'm doing the annual report for this household name. A few years ago I did some work for The Stock Exchange and again I felt it was very important.

"I think Hong Kong is a very creative place. Creativity is a gift from God and you can see it everywhere. Look at some households. They earn less than $10,000 a month but they raise five children and even send some of them to university. That's creativity of the highest level—minimum means but maximum effect."

What about artistic appreciation?

"Rome was not built in a day and taste is not built on money alone. Look at New Yorkers. On Sundays they go to churches or museums or art galleries— that's part of their culture. But in Hong Kong on Sunday most people go shopping, play mahjong, go horse racing or just sleep because they have been working so hard."

But John rejects the idea that Hong Kong's frenetic pace and hard nosed attitude make it a difficult place for artists.

"It's not an equation. I think New York is just as frantic, but look at their art and design. It would be an excuse if the standard of Hong Kong is not up to world standards because of the frantic pace. One can create in any field in any circumstance.

"Creativity is really getting in touch with your own self and bringing that out. Anyway, artists should reflect the spirit of where they are.

 "In some ways, I think Hong Kong has lost its momentum. Comparing us with designers from China, I think we are getting a little bit too successful. We've lost that kind of enthusiasm, that energy I saw here ten or twenty years ago—that hunger to create, that hunger to publish, that hunger to go to a seminar and listen to a German designer or a Japanese designer. I find Hong Kong these last couple of years almost like a middle-aged man, whereas Shenzhen or Beijing are like youths— they are so excited, so hungry."

John Au, approaching middle age himself, is a reflective, spiritual man. He has never seriously tried to build his business to the scale of Hong Kong's largest studios and recently spent a few months working alone with no staff at all, just to prove to himself that he could do it. He sets himself high professional standards, but also loves painting in a child's style with his two young sons. His ultimate interest is in a design for living.

"For me, that is especially true and clear. I want a very good life, meaning a balanced life. I position it in four sectors — personal growth, family and dear friends, career and giving back to the community. I don't think money is the end for me. It's the quality of life I'm looking for."

緬 懷 過 去

活 在 今 天

創 造 未 來

Learn from the past,

live in the present,

and create the future.

恭覺今古路

*Asking heaven
reverently what the
future holds.*

"Smell? The pig train from China."

"Eau de nullah."

"The smell of the hills after rain."

"Concrete canyons and a sense of claustrophobia—until I found the New Territories."

"Little old ladies collecting tin cans from rubbish bins."

"Gardening—from parks to pots. In this climate, it is impossible to fail."

"A wish? To establish the United Nations Asia Pacific Regional Headquarters in Hong Kong."

"A huge population of race-going gourmets who somehow find time for flower markets and moon watching."

Christine Loh
陸　恭　蕙

Ask Christine Loh what she likes about Hong Kong and you won't get any of the usual answers about eating, shopping or making money. The lady is a politician. "This is where I can be most effective in making changes," she says.

Are Hong Kong people really interested in politics?

"They're interested in issues. People tell me they're not interested in politics, but then they complain because their grandmother had to wait five hours to be seen in a public hospital, and I say there is obviously a problem of resource allocation, which is a political issue. You need to make the link.

"In terms of political awareness, we are at five out of ten. We now know what elections are, but the next quantum leap is to look at what elections mean. Who should really be running the government? What escaped me for many years is that elections are not really very meaningful if the elected representatives cannot govern."

Christine Loh was born into a wealthy family, spoke English as her first language, went off to boarding school in England and stayed there to study law. Strangely, although her father came from Shanghai, she cannot remember her parents ever talking about China—"it was on our doorstep but it could have been on another galaxy."

Years later a documentary film kindled her interest. She returned to Hong Kong, studied Mandarin for a year, went to work in Beijing for six months— "and fell in love with China." All thoughts of becoming a lawyer in England were forgotten. Instead, she became a commodities trader in Hong Kong, and began to take an interest in politics through the Hong Kong Observers.

"My life was a triangle— business, politics, arts. The other day I was looking at a speech I made in 1981,

saying Hong Kong was a cultural desert. Now, this still isn't London and it won't be for a long time because we don't yet have the breadth and depth of local people involved in the arts, but it's coming. There is now no shortage of original Cantonese plays we can go to, and just look at Phantom of the Opera or 'Les Mis' — they ran for weeks and weeks with packed audiences every night. Hong Kong people now like going to see things. That's a start."

The triangle of interests became a square when she started to focus on environmental issues. She was soon chairing Friends of the Earth and now believes passionately that the key to protecting Hong Kong's environment lies in coordinating local plans and policies with those for southern China.

"Ideas know no boundaries and nor, unfortunately, does pollution. The government's plan is to destroy the western side of Hong Kong and preserve the eastern side. But I've done a lot of sailing and walking on the eastern side and I tell you it's not going to work. There is so much development at Sha Tau Kok and it's very close to Hong Kong. We are not going to be able to keep Double Haven and those areas pristine."

But just when she was feeling depressed about Hong Kong's environmental future, Christine Loh met a whale.

"I was in Crescent Bay and it swam right by my boat. It was so beautiful, almost a religious experience. It was the defining moment in my life. Suddenly the provisional legislature didn't matter! I almost think that whale was saying to me: 'Yes, you're right to have a look at me because I'm not going to be here if this gets messed up.' So on the environment I just feel I must do everything I can.

"I want the Pearl River Delta, including parts of Fujian and Guangxi, this whole southern area, to be a much better planned area. We must not destroy by mistake or ignorance.

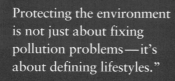

Protecting the environment is not just about fixing pollution problems—it's about defining lifestyles."

This concern for big, long-term issues is a hallmark of her work as a politician. She worries that Hong Kong lives from minute to minute, without a thought for what will happen in ten, twenty or fifty years' time.

"I genuinely feel like a member of Earth," she says. "Hong Kong can be so inward looking. People say that China is a quarter of the world's population. Well, yes, okay, but that means that three quarters are somewhere else."

It is hard to imagine Christine Loh anywhere else. She is clear that her future is as a politician in Hong Kong. Some people think she is mad. She thinks her time is coming.

"Even given the constraints of the Basic Law, there are ways for us to move forward," she says. "I am a politician. This is a new phenomenon in Hong Kong. I'm riding on a rising crest."

怨弦撥弄裕樂

Plucking strings for the pleasure of music.

"Hong Kong is a perfect place for friendships to flourish."

"It's difficult not to be attached to a place where you were born, went to school, worked and have lived all your life."

"The clatter and chink of china when tables are set in a restaurant."

"Noise. So many Hong Kong people shout rather than talk, even if they're only inches away from each other."

'Wai...Wai...Wai.'

"Hong Kong art? Stacking up a high salad in a bowl at Pizza Hut."

"I can't wait to leave. But when that time comes, it will be the saddest time I have ever experienced."

93

Simon Hui
許　裕　成

Simon Hui was born into a family which had just lost its fortune. His father died when he was a boy and a few years later his sister committed suicide. He passed up offers to study overseas because for twenty years he had to support his mother, finally caring for her through five years of Alzheimer's Disease.

"I'm glad you're talking to me today," he says with a smile. "Ten years ago I had so much frustration and anger. There were years and years when I

would look up into the sky and see a plane and say: 'I don't care where it's going, I just want to be on it.'"

Yet today Simon Hui describes himself as a lucky man. He is newly married and doing what he wants to do—playing double bass with the Hong Kong Philharmonic and the jazz trio, Han Shan.

His bass career began inauspiciously. He was happily learning classical guitar, but the school orchestra needed bass players and, as he was

taller than the other boys, he was forced to switch instruments.

"I absolutely hated it. It was so hard to hold the strings down—it was literally a pain to play. Even now I say to people that nobody in their right mind would play the double bass. It's just impossible."

But he had real talent and at the start of the 1987/88 season a friend urged him to audition for the Hong Kong Philharmonic, saying, "This is a Hong

Kong orchestra and you are from Hong Kong. You must do it." He passed the test and today is one of only a handful of Philharmonic players who were born and brought up in Hong Kong.

One month before joining the Philharmonic, he and a friend played their first jazz concert.

"It was supposed to be a one-off, but afterwards we decided that about one per

cent of it had been nice and so we got a piano player who could play chords and became a trio. That's how Han Shan was born."

He laughs. "I must have had some nerve to go up on stage and do what I did!" Yet ten years later, after a change of line-up, two CDs and many performances, Han Shan plays on.

"Classical music is saying somebody else's lines. In an orchestra, you are part of an instrument which the conductor plays and, unless you are given the freedom to do it, you don't inject your own personality. In jazz, people are applauding you, what you said.

"By far my favourite place to perform is the Fringe Theatre because you are so close to the audience. You get so much from the audience and it goes back into the music. That's when you really feel something

personal, whereas in an orchestra most of the time you just feel functional.

"But they are different situations and I don't see any tension between them. When you are in your shower, you don't cut your birthday cake."

Simon's musical tastes and interests are diverse. Apart from his double bass, he plays ethnic flutes and teaches cello. He has started a small company, doing everything from composing

to recording. Yet he lacks a deep understanding of his own Chinese culture — the result, he says, of attending an Anglo-Chinese school.

"We had a string orchestra trying to play Tchaikovsky, but I knew nothing about Chinese history or Chinese literature, and today I really feel ashamed about that. I try to listen more to traditional Chinese music, but I don't think it's going to get into my system."

Then he runs his hand through his hair and reflects on the irony that most Chinese people do not appreciate his music.

"Do Hong Kong people want to be more appreciative?" he wonders. "After long hours of work, do they want to listen to a ninety-minute Mahler symphony? Wouldn't they prefer a three-minute Aaron Kwok song? Although I'm a classical musician, I don't say that everyone should know their Shostakovitchs. To the guy in the street, all he wants is something that he can move to and relax to.

"I don't like it when people who enjoy Canto-pop say to me: 'Oh, I'm not up to your level.' I don't think it's a question of levels. There are just different areas of music."

The tolerance of a man finally at ease with himself and his music. Simon Hui at thirty-eight. Mellow.

憂民苦今惜生

Concerns for the people
rise in the mind.

"No matter which way you walk down the street, everyone is walking against you."

"First impression? So overcrowded. And that was 1963!"

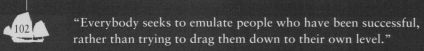

"Everybody seeks to emulate people who have been successful, rather than trying to drag them down to their own level."

"The people. They are great!"

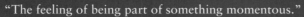

"The feeling of being part of something momentous."

"People walking quickly."

"Old people playing chess in a park."

"Generosity on Saturdays when charities make their street collections—and even more when there is a special disaster."

Christine Fang
方　敏　生

Christine Fang grew up in a large house beside the beach in Stanley. She and her five brothers and sisters played in the garden and splashed in the pool. Stanley was then a small fishing community and the children knew all the lifeguards on the beach and the stallholders in the market.

"I remember going to the Chinese opera in the village with the amahs, running around backstage and getting introduced to all the singers. They looked so beautiful in their costumes."

It was a rich and loving home. Every festival was celebrated in style and tutors came to the house to teach her sewing and cooking. There were trips to the United States and Europe. Her parents recognised the value of a broad education.

"It was," she says, "a lovely childhood."

Then she discovered how the other half lives. She left the comfort of home and moved into a hostel at the University of Hong Kong to study social work. She threw herself into student activities, studied philosophy in her spare time and became a social activist.

One summer she worked in a drug rehabilitation centre for prostitutes in Wan Chai, with women

who were old enough to be her mother, women who had been abused and were often deeply in debt. She learned not to categorise people but to appreciate them, not to judge but to try to help.

As her own younger brother and sisters debated whether to study in Europe or the States, whether to do medicine or accounting, she worked with youngsters from criminal gangs, whose prospects were rather more bleak.

Her first full-time job was on a community development project for young workers at a temporary housing area in Lei Cheng Uk— "the first time I got to go to a place in Kowloon other than the airport and

Ocean Terminal." The residents were angry about a government proposal to increase their rents.

"A temporary housing area in those days was almost like a licensed squatter area. The government just put up a roof. The people even had to put up the walls on their own. The toilets were so dirty, and the government charged people for a kitchen even though they didn't have a kitchen. How could they increase the rent?

"The first time I'd been to a public housing estate was with my maths tutor. I remember thinking that the whole flat, including the kitchen, including everything, was just the size of my room at home."

Middle-aged prostitutes, young tearaways, poor working families—they taught the young social worker about injustice but they also showed her how remarkably resilient Hong Kong people are.

"What I like about Hong Kong is the people. They are good at living in difficult situations. Even now, with this 1997 situation, you can feel this affinity between us Hong Kong people."

Today, Christine Fang is Secretary General of the Hong Kong Red Cross. The former grassroots social worker and community organiser is overseeing a wide range of health, welfare and education

services and a force of 10,000 volunteers. She is a charming, smiling, dynamic woman, living back in Stanley with her husband and two children. She has become experienced at

negotiating with government and handling the frustrations and politics of a large organisation. She is, if you like, a modern manager.

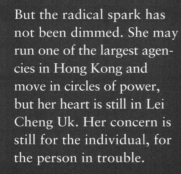

But the radical spark has not been dimmed. She may run one of the largest agencies in Hong Kong and move in circles of power, but her heart is still in Lei Cheng Uk. Her concern is still for the individual, for the person in trouble.

Is Hong Kong today a just society?

She thinks for a long time, then says quietly: "No. People like to believe it is. Even people who are unfairly treated like to believe it is, because it gives them hope. It seems that if you can complete nine years of free education and get a job, you can work it through, but how many people can really go up this ladder? It's not fair in terms of the failure rate."

She is thinking of all those people at the margins of society—new immigrants from China, children from single parent families, teenagers in trouble with triads, people who have missed out on Hong Kong's prosperity and who still live in grinding poverty.

"Hong Kong is not a country, we have no rights. Hong Kong is a home, and in a home what matters most are the people."

Acknowledgements

Many people have made important contributions to this book.

Most of the photographs were taken by Tim Nutt, John Lambon and Ian Stevens. Others were by courtesy of: Cheung Chi Wai (pp. 97–99, double bass jazz scenes), Pixie Thomas (p. 51, sailing scenes), Golden Harvest (International) Limited (pp. 52–55, Jackie Chan action scenes), the Government Information Services (pp. 42, 43, 45, N.T. rural scenes, Shatin Valley, 1950s), The Hong Kong Jockey Club (pp. 49, 50, the Mark Six Lottery,

horse racing and racing newspapers), Hong Kong Philharmonic Orchestra (p. 96, the orchestra), and The Hongkong and Shanghai Banking Corporation Limited (p. 49, view of vault door, Head Office).

John Au, Chung Wah Nan and Fang Zhaoling all contributed original artworks. Chung Wah Nan also wrote the Chinese verse and did the calligraphy for the theme opening pages. Forty children from schools run by Hong Kong Red Cross and The Hong Kong Association for the Mentally Handicapped contributed original paintings.

Sir David Akers-Jones, John Au, Jackie Chan, Chung Wah Nan, Christine Fang, Fang Zhaoling, Simon Hui, Doris Lau, Leung Kwok Lin Choi and Christine Loh all gave generously of their time and ideas. Hundreds more friends, whose names are listed below, contributed ideas and comments which inspired the photographs.

The authors also gratefully acknowledge the assistance and support of Valeria Nutt and the Chinese University Press team.

The following friends all contributed ideas to this book:

Anisa Abdoolcarim
Ileana and Roberto Adam
John and Marina Adams
Lev Adams
Father Jose Serafin Anaya
Joanlin Au

Ian and Ann Bagshaw
Randal and Mary Bale
Collette and Oliver Barnham
Ray and Catherine Bates
Chris and Valentina Beggs
Gelinde Behr-Johansen
Bill and Andrin Blaauw
Rocio Blasco-Gardner
John Bottomley
Natalie Bown
Ceridwen and John Brinkers
Maggie and Nicholas Brooke
David and Socorro Browning
Nick Burns
Julie Burrows
Ian and Theresa Butler

Bessie Cagney
John Cagney
Ann and Robin Carpenter
Doug Castledine
Steve Chamberlain

Lowell and Phyllis Chan
Colin and Antoinette Chan-Pensley
Carol Charlton
Anthony and Tony Charter
Carolyn and William Chen
Cheng Chi Wah
Sherman Yuen Ching Cheng
Albert Cheung
Andy W S Cheung
Eric and Maria Guadalupe Cheung
Waverly Y W Chin
John Y N Chiu
France Choa
Edward Christopher
Chu Toi Chi
Annette and Colin Crisswell

Bente Dahl
Ulrika Dalen
Bertie de Speville
Joyce and Nigel Digges
Joseph and Pat Duffy

Dot and Tony Elliott
Graham and Wendy Eckersley

David and Patricia Fergusson
Sophie and Paul Fermin
Father Carlos Fernandez
Ruth Franco
Nigel French
Billy Fung

Chris and Linda Gabriel
Mark W Gardiner
Simon Greensted
Glenda Gomez de Lalwani
Darcy and Marie Glossop
Fiona and Gordon Gregor
Ric Grosvenor

Martin Hadaway
Ross and Stuart Hall
Bill Hamblet
Clive and Kate Hardman
David Hedges
Cynthia and Jim Henderson
Tao Ho
John Holdaway
Gemma and Phil Holmes
Robin Howes
Richard Hownam-Meek
Lilly Hui

Maria-Paz and Moon Wai Ip
Jacob and Liz Izbiki

Jenny and Peter Jagodzinsky
Jeanette and Mike Johnson
David and Hilary Jolliffe

Rosann Kao
Margot Keen
Bob Kessler
Celia and Horst Kleinwechter

Bob and Lesley Knight
Joanna Knight
Dadrey Ko
Andy S K Kok
Tokashi Komatsu
Rick Kroos
Thomas Kwok

Michael Lam
Peter Lam
John and Celia Lambon
Ian Lambot
Tom Larmour
Howard and Linda Lazenby
Tunney Lee
Lupe Lee
Jo and Marta Lei
Andy K M Leung
Phoenix Pui Fung Leung
Philip Yuen Yam Li
Scott Ligertwood
Mark Lloyd-Williams
Vic Locke
Eric Lockyear
Ray Logan
Mariati Lucas
Betty and Tony Lui
Maggie and Michael Lunn
Sarah Lunn

Martin Magill
Derek Messling

Tony Miller
Elizabeth and Rodney Minns
Ezequiel and Gilda Morones
David Morris
Ray Morris
Stephanie Morton
Sweeta Motwani
Liz and Roger Muscroft

Merce Neilson
Jackie and Roger North
David Nutt
Simone Nutt

T Oguri
David and Margaret Openshaw
Adriana and Mark Osborn
Virginia Owen

Jeronime Palmer
Allan Parry
Charles Picken
Alan and Jo Potts
Emma Potts
Ken and Lynne Prangnell
David Puller
Susan and William Pye

Mike Quinn

Bob and Ginger Rees
Antonio Represas

Val Richards
David Roberts
Alan Ruxton

Jean and Tony Samson
Dee Saunders
Paul and Pauline Savage
Sonia Sawyer
Paul Sayer
Leslie Simon
Almon Po Wai Sin
Terry Smith
Bonnie Y H So
Helen Solitario
Richard and Trish Steil
Ian and Lysbeth Stevens
Bob and Moira Storey
Marina Chirolla Stubbs
Brian Sullivan
Neil Sutherland

C T Tam
Beatriz Tancock
Pixie Thomas
Les Thompson
Tony C S Toh
Carlton Tropper
Iris and Nigel Travers-Griffin
Barry Sun Nam Tsang
Mary Tse

Kenji Ueda

Sheila Venville
Simon Vickers
Steve Vine

Carole Wadham
Graham Walker
Rebeca Ulloa Walker
Arthur Wall
Penny Ward
Neil and Araceli Wiseman
Billy Wong
Helen and Steve K C Wong
John and Portia Wong
Nora Wong
Steve C S Wong
Winnie Wai Shuen Wong
Winnie Sau Ling Wong
Hugh S H Wu

Michael Yu

Vivian Zee

Photographs